DAILY XCELLENCE

It's your responsibility

YOU ARE WHERE YOUR FEET ARE

BY KEVIN CRAGGS

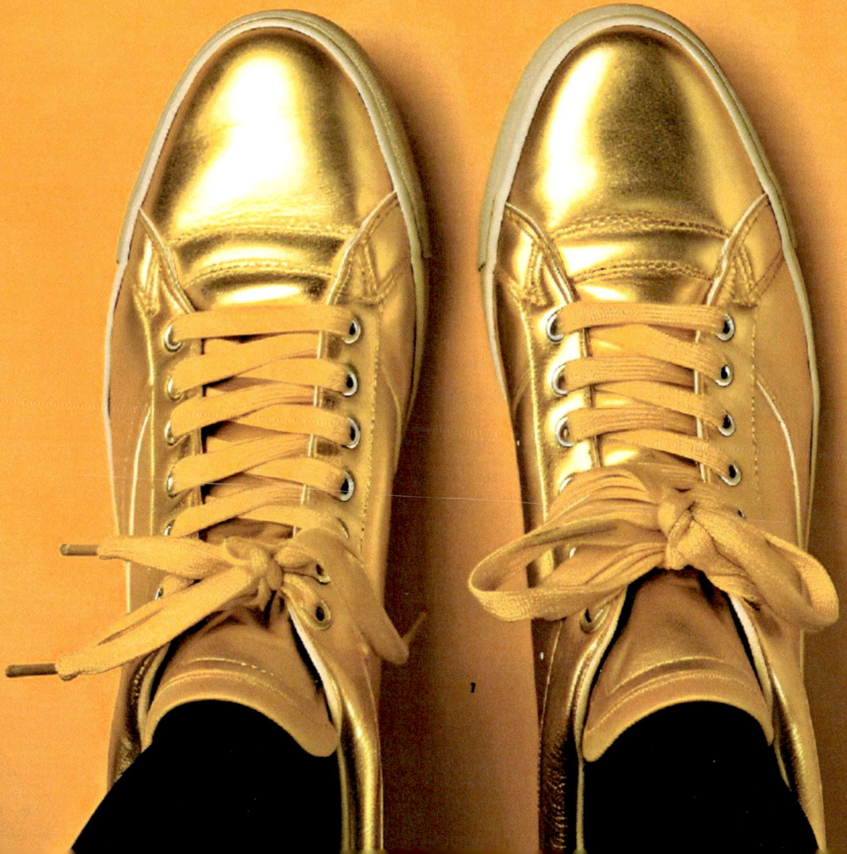

INTRODUCTION TO
"YOU ARE WHERE YOUR FEET ARE"

Welcome to "You Are Where Your Feet Are" – your daily companion for personal excellence. The idea for this book came from my beloved granny. As a youngster full of ambition and mischief, I would often say, "I can't wait until…" or "I remember when I could…" She would always stop me and remind me, "You are where your feet are." This simple statement encouraged me to focus on the present rather than always looking ahead or dwelling on the past. It profoundly impacted my life and career.

In my coaching career, working with top athletes and business leaders, this phrase became the backbone of my philosophy. Its guided individuals in managing the distractions of business, performance pressures, or everyday life, bringing them back to the present moment.

This book provides quick and actionable challenges that you can select at random. These challenges are designed to improve your self-awareness, time management, resilience, and more. Simply open the book, choose a challenge, and take it on for the day. There's no need to read in order – just dive in where you feel inspired. Each challenge is fun, fast, and easy to implement, helping you make small, positive changes that lead to significant personal growth.

Recognizing where you are and maximizing each moment is key. This book is designed to be enjoyable, easy to read, and quick to apply, helping you build better habits and develop behaviors of excellence.

Remember, "You Are Where Your Feet Are," and right now, you are here, reading this book.

Kevin Craggs

HOW TO USE THIS BOOK

To enhance your experience with 'You Are Where Your Feet Are,' we've designed this book to be interactive. Each challenge page can be torn out once you've completed the task. This physical act serves as a symbol of your progress and a reminder of the steps you're taking towards personal excellence.

PICK A CHALLENGE: Open the book to any page and choose a challenge that speaks to you. This allows you to focus on what resonates most with you at the moment.

TAKE ACTION: Follow the instructions and complete the challenge for the day. Each task is designed to be quick and easy to implement.

TEAR OUT THE PAGE: Once finished, tear out the page to provide you with a sense of accomplishment. This physical act marks your progress.

REFLECT: Use the reference guide at the back to revisit and reflect on all the challenges you've completed. This helps reinforce your growth and learning.

REFLECTION NOTES AND REFERENCE GUIDE

REFLECTION NOTES:

Use this section at the back of the book to jot down your thoughts, experiences, and learnings from each challenge. This will help you track your growth and revisit your experiences whenever needed.

REFERENCE GUIDE:

For your convenience, the Reference Guide located at the back provides a quick summary of each challenge. If you've torn out the page but want to revisit the challenge, refer back here for a reminder of what each task entailed.

ABOUT THE AUTHOR

Kevin Craggs is a globally renowned PGA Professional with nearly four decades of coaching experience. He has coached and mentored major championship winners, Ryder Cup and Solheim Cup players, and some of the world's top business leaders and royalty. His unique motivational style and technical expertise have made him one of the most sought-after coaches in golf.

Kevin's career highlights include coaching legends like two-time major winner Sandy Lyle and Colin Montgomerie, who has won a record eight European Tour Order of Merit titles, as well as major winners Catriona Matthew and Paula Creamer. With over 50,000 hours of coaching across all major tours worldwide, Kevin has earned recognition as one of Golf Monthly's Top 25 Coaches. He also cherished memorable moments learning from and being mentored by the legendary Seve Ballesteros.

Kevin's passion lies in helping others excel. Leveraging his high-performance golf coaching techniques, he has successfully transitioned into leadership coaching for leaders and executives. Kevin's practical courses provide strategies for success in both business and life, changing behaviors through a proven coaching system.

Kevin is also the founder of Daily Xcellence, a platform dedicated to transforming coaches, trainers, and leaders through reflective learning and self-discovery. Daily Xcellence offers comprehensive coaching systems, personalized development programs, and international certification.

Enjoy this interactive book—it's fun to read, easy to grasp, and simple to put into action. Use it to develop daily excellence habits and behaviors.

TESTIMONIALS

"Kevin's passion to coach and his energy are contagious. He really knows his stuff and gives you the confidence to improve. He's a great coach who always pushes you to get better."

Sandy Lyle
Multiple Tour Winner & Two-Time Major Winner

"Kevin is the most enthusiastic and positive coach I've ever had. He is terrific and has vast knowledge."

Colin Montgomerie
Eight-Time Order of Merit Winner, Multiple Tour Winner, Nine Ryder Cups & Ryder Cup Winning Captain

"One of the most natural and talented coaches I have ever seen."

Severiano Ballesteros
Multiple Tour Winner & Five-Time Major Winner

"Kevin has been a very positive influence on my golf both mentally and physically. His great attitude and work on my game had me playing the best golf of my life."

Catriona Matthew
LPGA Tour Winner, Major Winner, Eight Solheim Cups and Two-Time Winning Solheim Cup Captain

"Kevin not only saved my game but also rescued my career. His world-class knowledge and simple coaching approach are major influences on me on and off the course."

Mel Reid
Multiple Tour Winner on LET & LPGA

NOTE ON TRANSFERABILITY

The coaching principles that have transformed the careers of these elite athletes are the same principles Kevin applies to his broader coaching programs. Whether in sports, business, or personal development, Kevin's methods are designed to help individuals excel and achieve their full potential.

CONTENTS

CONTENTS

NAVIGATE UNCERTAINTY: FIND YOUR PATH

Life is full of unknowns. Embrace uncertainty as an opportunity to explore new directions and opportunities. Trust yourself to navigate challenges with resilience and determination. Uncertainty often brings the greatest potential for growth and discovery, pushing you out of your comfort zone.

CHALLENGE:

Identify one area of uncertainty in your life. List possible paths forward and consider the potential outcomes of each. Choose one step you can take today to clarify your direction and reduce your uncertainty. Embrace the process and acknowledge the confidence and skills you gain along the way.

EMBRACE CHANGE: ADAPT & GROW

Change is inevitable and often challenging, but it's an important part of growth and learning. Embrace change as an opportunity to learn new things and discover new strengths. Staying flexible and open-minded allows you to navigate transitions with confidence and commitment.

CHALLENGE:

Reflect on a recent change you've faced. Identify one positive aspect or opportunity it has brought. Write down how you adapted and what you learned from the experience. Commit to embracing future changes with a positive mindset, recognizing that every change brings new opportunities for growth.

DISCOVER PURPOSE: FIND MEANING

Purpose gives life direction and meaning, acting as a compass in your journey. Reflect on your passions and values to uncover what truly matters to you. Aligning your actions with your purpose allows you to live with greater intention and fulfillment, making everyday tasks more meaningful.

CHALLENGE:

Take some time to write down what brings you happiness and satisfaction. Reflect on the moments when you feel most alive and engaged. Identify how these moments align with your core values. Choose a small action today that aligns with your purpose and brings you closer to your goals. Notice the difference in your motivation and satisfaction when your actions are purpose-driven.

PRACTICE PATIENCE: TAKE IT STEP BY STEP

Patience is a virtue that builds discipline, resilience, and self-control. Embrace patience as you work towards your goals and intentions, knowing that true progress takes time, effort, and consistency. Each step, no matter how small, is a part of taking steps in the right direction.

CHALLENGE:

Identify one of your goals or intentions. Break it into smaller, manageable tasks. Each day, focus on completing just one task without rushing and while managing distractions. Reflect on how this simple routine helps you stay on track, feel in control, and provides you with a sense of purpose and achievement. Recognize that patience in the process leads to long-term success.

"*PATIENCE IS NOT THE ABILITY TO WAIT, BUT THE ABILITY TO KEEP A GOOD ATTITUDE WHILE WAITING.*"

—————

JOYCE MEYER

SHOW GRATITUDE: APPRECIATE EACH STEP

Gratitude is a powerful practice that enhances your perspective and well-being. By recognizing and appreciating the small wins and achievements in your life, you can cultivate a more positive and fulfilling mindset. Gratitude opens your heart and enriches your experiences.

CHALLENGE:

Each day, tell someone three things you're grateful for. Reflect on how sharing these moments of gratitude influences your perspective and positively impacts theirs. Consider keeping a gratitude journal to document these moments and revisit them when you need a boost. Notice how a consistent practice of gratitude improves your overall outlook on life.

BUILD RELATIONSHIPS: CONNECT WITH OTHERS

Strong relationships are essential for personal growth and happiness. Take the time to nurture meaningful connections with family, friends, and colleagues. These bonds provide support, encouragement, and a genuine sense of connection.

CHALLENGE:

Reach out to someone you haven't spoken to in a while. Set a time to catch up, reconnect, and strengthen your relationship. Consider asking meaningful questions to deepen your understanding of each other. Reflect on how this renewed connection brings mutual benefits and improves your overall happiness. Notice how investing in relationships strengthens your support network and personal well-being.

MANAGE STRESS: LIGHTEN YOUR LOAD

Stress is a natural part of life, but managing it well is crucial for your well-being and optimizing your performance. Stress often impacts us without us even realizing it, with poor sleep being one of the first signs. Recognizing and addressing stress is key to maintaining balance and health.

CHALLENGE:

Identify one source of stress in your life. Determine if it is within your control. If it is, develop a specific strategy to reduce its impact, such as setting clear boundaries, delegating tasks, or incorporating regular exercise, which is proven to be one of the most powerful ways to reduce anxiety and stress. If it's beyond your control, focus on changing your attitude towards it. Implement these changes and observe how they reduce your stress, improving your overall well-being and perspective.

BE OPEN-MINDED: EMBRACE DIVERSITY

Diversity enriches our perspectives and strengthens communities. The world is constantly changing and evolving, and we must move with it by being open-minded to different cultures, beliefs, and opinions. Facing challenges to our beliefs and values can be beneficial because it promotes learning and growth. Remember, 'Everyone has two eyes, but no one has the same view.' Wouldn't a world where everyone looked and behaved the same be boring?

CHALLENGE:

Engage in conversations with people from different backgrounds. Listen actively, seeking to understand their experiences and viewpoints. Reflect on how these interactions broaden your perspective, develop mutual respect, and help you navigate an ever-evolving world.

TAKE INITIATIVE: TAKE ACTION

Initiative is the key to turning ambitions and intentions into reality. The world is full of opportunities, but it's up to you to seize them. Be proactive and take responsibility for creating the life you desire. Remember, waiting for things to happen won't get you where you want to be.

CHALLENGE:

Identify one area in your life where you've been waiting for things to happen. Take the first step today toward making progress in that area. Break it down into manageable tasks and set clear goals. Establish small benchmarks as signposts, ensuring you're heading in the right direction. It's no different from using Google Maps: you set a destination, and it provides various routes and timelines. If you go off course, don't panic—re-route and stay focused on your direction. Reflect on how taking initiative helps you gain control and move closer to your ambitions and intentions."

STORIES THAT LEAVE A FOOTPRINT

STORY 1: *TAKING INITIATIVE*

I was fortunate to spend golden moments with rugby star Jonah Lomu. This All Blacks Rugby legend, widely regarded as one of the greatest and most influential players in the history of the sport, stood at 6 feet 4 inches and weighed 265 pounds. Jonah's fierce and chilled exterior concealed a man filled with genuine kindness and gratitude.

In one of our conversations, he shared a powerful story that continues to resonate with me—a tale that imparts a profound lesson on resilience and self-worth. During a halftime locker room talk, the head coach delivered a poignant message to the players. He reminded them that the jersey they wear is borrowed, symbolizing a pride and culture greater than each individual wearing it.

The story unfolds as the coach tells of a young man attempting to make the All Blacks team. On his first attempt, he returns home disappointed, but his father wisely says, "Just one man's opinion." The pattern repeats, but the father's response remains the same. Finally, after two years, the young man succeeds, proudly holding the prestigious All Blacks jersey. Yet his father, with a knowing smile, repeats, "Just one man's opinion."

This narrative stands as a testament to the resilience embedded in the human spirit and reinforces the invaluable concept of self-worth. It serves as a poignant reminder that our true value is not defined by the opinions of others. Instead, it comes from within, reflecting the unbeatable spirit that drives us forward in the face of challenges.

Lesson: True resilience and self-worth come from within, not from the opinions of others.

Footprint: "You Are Where Your Feet Are" — your current actions and beliefs about yourself shape your journey and define your path to success.

"*THE BEST WAY TO PREDICT THE FUTURE IS TO CREATE IT.*"

———

PETER DRUCKER

DEVELOP RESILIENCE: BOUNCE BACK STRONGER

Resilience is the ability to recover from setbacks with strength and determination. Setbacks often prepare the stage for comebacks, allowing you to face adversity and emerge even stronger. Build resilience by becoming self-aware and developing adaptive coping strategies, focusing on the present challenges you face.

CHALLENGE:

Reflect on a recent challenge or setback you experienced. Identify one valuable lesson you learned from it. Write down how you can apply this lesson to handle future challenges more effectively and bounce back even stronger. Notice how this approach helps you build resilience and prepares you for future comebacks.

SEEK BALANCE: FIND HARMONY

Balance is essential for achieving an optimal state where you can build, learn, and grow. Finding harmony between work, relationships, personal growth, and relaxation allows you to perform at your best in all areas of life. Being mindful of where you are right now helps maintain balance in your daily life.

CHALLENGE:

Take a moment to assess your current schedule and commitments. Identify one area where you feel imbalanced. Write down one specific adjustment you can make to create more balance and harmony in your life. It could be setting aside time for relaxation, prioritizing personal growth, or dedicating more time to relationships. Reflect on how this adjustment can positively impact your ability to build, learn, and grow.

CREATIVITY: EXPLORE IDEAS

Creativity fuels innovation and personal growth. If you're not curious, you're not creative. Curiosity is the foundation of creativity, allowing you to explore new ideas and perspectives. Engage in activities that inspire and challenge your imagination, focusing on the creative opportunities present in your current environment.

CHALLENGE:

Dedicate time each week to explore a creative hobby or project. Allow yourself to experiment and embrace the process without judgment. Reflect on how this creative exploration enhances your curiosity and leads to new insights and personal growth. Remember, if you're not learning, you're not growing.

COMMUNICATION: UNDERSTAND AND BE UNDERSTOOD

Effective communication is essential for building strong relationships and achieving shared goals. It involves both listening attentively and expressing yourself clearly. Remember, it's not always what you say but how you say it. Good communication helps to bridge gaps and enhance collaboration.

CHALLENGE:

Choose one relationship or situation where clear communication is crucial. Practice active listening by giving your full attention, avoiding interruptions, and asking clarifying questions to ensure mutual understanding. Notice how these efforts improve your interactions and help achieve better outcomes.

INTEGRITY:
BE HONEST & TRUE

Integrity builds trust and respect. Lead by example with honesty, authenticity, and consistency in your actions and decisions. Being true to your values and principles strengthens your character and influence, making you a reliable and trustworthy individual.

CHALLENGE:

Reflect on your core values. Identify one situation where you can demonstrate integrity through your actions today. Consider how this choice aligns with your principles and impacts those around you. Notice how acting with integrity enhances your relationships, reinforces your self-respect, and sets a positive example for others.

"INTEGRITY IS DOING
THE RIGHT THING,
EVEN WHEN NO ONE
IS WATCHING."

———————

C.S. LEWIS

INSPIRE OTHERS: MOTIVATE AND ENCOURAGE

Your words and actions have the power to inspire and uplift others. By sharing positivity and encouragement, you can help other people excel and reach their full potential. Remember, "You Are Where Your Feet Are," and your presence can make a difference in someone's life.

CHALLENGE:

Identify someone in your life who could use some support or inspiration. Reach out to them with a thoughtful message, offering words of encouragement or sharing a story of perseverance. Follow up to see how they're doing and continue to provide support. Reflect on how your efforts to help others excel not only uplift them but also bring a sense of purpose and fulfillment to your own life.

CELEBRATE SUCCESS: ACKNOWLEDGE ACHIEVEMENTS

Celebrating success reinforces positive behavior and boosts morale. It's important to take time to acknowledge and celebrate both your own achievements and those of others. Recognizing success helps to build confidence and motivation. Desire and drive need to be fueled with rewards, as they hold the key to being consistent and drive enthusiasm to learn more and become more.

CHALLENGE:

Reflect on a recent accomplishment, no matter how small. Treat yourself to a small reward or share your success with someone who supports you. Notice how this celebration boosts your morale and fuels your desire and drive for further achievements.

LEARN FROM FAILURE: GROW FROM MISTAKES

Failure is an opportunity for growth and learning. Embrace mistakes as valuable lessons that pave the way to success. Remember, "You Are Where Your Feet Are," and just as easily as you stepped into failure, you can step out of it by using it as a valuable learning moment.

CHALLENGE:

Think of a recent failure or mistake. Identify one key lesson you've learned from it. Consider how you can apply this knowledge to improve your future actions and decisions. Reflect on how this shift in perspective transforms failure into a stepping stone for success and helps you move forward.

STORIES THAT LEAVE A FOOTPRINT

STORY 2: *LEARNING FROM FAILURE*

Throughout my career, I've been fortunate to coach many people, but one of the most personal experiences involved my son, Ben. A Scottish internationalist, Ben represented his country multiple times before turning professional at 18. His early successes showcased his undeniable talent, but he often got caught up in over analyzing his swing, losing focus on the simple things and misdirecting his energy.

After a series of events, Ben's lack of trust and confidence led to a significant setback. Disheartened and frustrated, he didn't know how to move forward. Seeking guidance, we had a long conversation about channelling his efforts correctly and viewing failure as a learning opportunity.

I explained that true progress comes from perseverance and dedication—not shortcuts or quick fixes. I encouraged him to see his setback as a chance to grow. Ben took this advice to heart, dedicating himself to quality work, accountability, and focusing on what truly mattered.

Over the following months, his performance steadily improved. He became more disciplined, resilient, and determined. Eventually, his efforts paid off, and he not only regained his competitive edge but also developed a deeper appreciation for the growth process.

This experience taught us both a valuable lesson: success isn't just about results, but about the journey of continuous improvement and learning from failures.

Lesson: **Real growth comes from genuine effort and learning from setbacks, not quick fixes.**

Footprint: **"You Are Where Your Feet Are"—your current dedication and honesty in facing challenges define your path to success.**

"SUCCESS IS NOT
FINAL, FAILURE IS
NOT FATAL: IT IS
THE COURAGE TO
CONTINUE THAT
COUNTS."

———

WINSTON CHURCHILL

NURTURE COMPASSION: BE KIND TO YOURSELF

Self-compassion is essential for mental and emotional well-being. Treat yourself with the same kindness and understanding you would offer to a friend. Acknowledge your struggles without judgment and offer yourself support and encouragement. Being present includes being kind to yourself, recognizing your worth, and giving yourself the grace to grow.

CHALLENGE:

Notice self-critical thoughts throughout your day. When you catch yourself being self-critical, pause and replace those thoughts with words of self-compassion and reassurance. Dedicate time to self-care activities that nourish your mind and body, such as meditation, exercise, or spending time in nature. Reflect on how treating yourself with kindness enhances your overall physical and mental state, allowing you to navigate life's challenges with greater ease.

CHALLENGE ASSUMPTIONS: QUESTION WHAT YOU KNOW

Challenging assumptions develops critical thinking and innovation. By questioning what you know, you open up new possibilities for growth and understanding. It encourages you to look beyond the obvious and explore new perspectives. This process can also confirm that what you know is correct or expand your knowledge.

CHALLENGE:

Identify a belief or assumption you hold. Seek out different perspectives or research to gain a broader understanding of the topic. Reflect on how this new information changes your view, confirms your beliefs, or expands your knowledge, contributing to your personal growth.

"*THE GREATEST ENEMY OF KNOWLEDGE IS NOT IGNORANCE, IT IS THE ILLUSION OF KNOWLEDGE.*"

STEPHEN HAWKING

CHOOSE COURAGE: BE BRAVE

Courage is about facing fears and challenges with bravery and determination. Stepping outside your comfort zone is essential for growth and achieving your goals. Embracing courage allows you to take risks and explore new possibilities. It's through courageous actions that we discover our true potential and expand our opportunities.

CHALLENGE:

Identify a fear or concern you've been avoiding. Take one small step today to confront or overcome it. This could be as simple as having a difficult conversation, trying something new, or taking the first step towards a big goal. Reflect on how this act of bravery impacts your confidence and moves you closer to your goals. Consider how each courageous step builds your resilience and opens doors to new opportunities.

REFLECT REGULARLY: PAUSE AND CONTEMPLATE

Reflection enhances self-awareness and personal growth. It's not always easy and can often feel unfamiliar and uncomfortable. Looking at yourself directly in the mirror and giving yourself advice is a powerful exercise to understand this. By regularly pausing to contemplate your experiences, you gain valuable insights for the future.

CHALLENGE:

Schedule regular reflection time, whether weekly or monthly. Use this time to write down your thoughts, experiences, and lessons learned. This practice will deepen your self-awareness and help you navigate your intentions with greater clarity and purpose. Reflect on how these insights can guide your actions and decisions, helping you to grow and improve continually.

TAKE CONTROL: MOVE YOUR FEET TO WHERE THEY NEED TO BE

Own your decisions and take charge of where you are in life. Whether you're starting something new, making a career change, or tackling a long-standing goal, your actions shape your path. Procrastination can hold you back, but decisive action moves you forward. Remember the saying, 'Why put off till tomorrow what can be done today'—you control your thoughts, choices, and actions, so start moving your feet to where they need to be today.

CHALLENGE:

Identify one area of your life where you feel stuck. Write down three small steps you can take to move forward. Commit to taking the first step. Taking control of your decisions empowers you and sets you on the path to achieving your goals. You'll quickly notice how each step builds momentum, making it easier to continue moving forward.

STORIES THAT LEAVE A FOOTPRINT

STORY 3: *THE HILL*

This impactful story was shared with me by my great friend Dwight Thomas, an Olympic gold medalist who was a member of the Jamaican relay team. Dwight described Jamaica's undeveloped training facilities, where sheer determination, sweat, and hard work replaced fancy equipment ahead of Olympic Games preparations.

During a mid-afternoon training session, the coach directed the team to sprint up a steep hill and walk back down, repeating the cycle countless times. As the coach shouted from the sidelines to push harder and move quicker, Dwight turned to his teammate Usain Bolt and asked, "Do you think this hill is making us stronger or faster?" Bolt replied, "I don't know. Why not ask the coach?" Dwight approached the coach at the bottom of the hill and asked, "Coach, is this hill making us stronger?" The coach laughed and replied, "No, man." Dwight repeated, "Coach, is this hill making us faster?" The coach chuckled again, saying, "No, man." At that moment, the entire team looked up and questioned, "Why are we running the hill then?" The coach, standing up from the shade, pointed to them and declared, "Because no one else is."

Fast forward to the Olympic Games. As the Jamaican team looked around the track before the final of the 4x100 relay, they knew every competitor had dedicated years to being among the fastest in the world. But none had run the hill - a unique edge that drove the team to victory, securing the gold medal.

Lesson: **Overcoming challenging obstacles builds resilience and prepares you for greater challenges ahead. The unique challenges you face and overcome give you an edge that others do not have.**

Footprint: **"You Are Where Your Feet Are" - how you face and overcome challenges in the present shapes your resilience for the future.**

"*THE GREATER THE OBSTACLE, THE MORE GLORY IN OVERCOMING IT*".

——————

MOLIERE

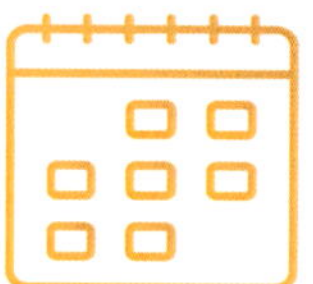

PREPARE FOR SUCCESS: PLAN AHEAD

Success is about clarity, commitment, and composure. Instead of asking, "What's the worst that could happen if it went wrong?" ask yourself, "What's the best that could happen if it went to plan?" Preparing for success involves being clear on your intentions, committing to them no matter what, and maintaining your emotions through the highs and lows of the journey.

CHALLENGE:

Identify one goal you want to achieve. Write down your clear intention for this goal, the steps you need to commit to, and how you will maintain your emotions throughout the process. Set simple milestones to keep you focused and encouraged that you are moving in the right direction. Notice how this preparation builds your confidence and keeps you motivated to achieve the best possible outcome.

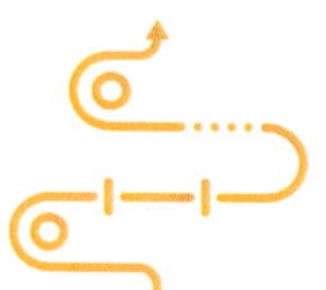

TRUST THE PROCESS: BELIEVE IN THE JOURNEY

We all like the idea of change and success, but sticking to the process and seeing it through is often a different matter. You can achieve anything you set your mind to, provided you hold strong in believing and committing to the process required to get you where you want to be.

CHALLENGE:

Identify one task or intention you have. Break it down into small, manageable chunks. Remember the old saying, "How do you eat an elephant? One bite at a time." If the task is too big, the process to get there can become overwhelming. Focus on completing one small step at a time. Notice how this approach makes the process more manageable and keeps you motivated to see it through to the end.

INVEST IN YOURSELF: PERSONAL GROWTH

The best investment you will ever make is in yourself. Prioritizing your time and energy in investing in your health, family, personal growth, and career is essential. Too often, we overlook our own investment, but it is critical for boosting confidence, creating opportunities, facilitating change, and maintaining mental health.

CHALLENGE:

Identify one area of your life where you can invest more in yourself. It could be your health, learning a new skill, spending quality time with family, or advancing your career. Dedicate time and resources to this area, even if it's just a small step each day. Pay attention to how this investment boosts your confidence, opens up new opportunities, and positively impacts your overall well-being.

LEAVE A POSITIVE FOOTPRINT: INSPIRE AND EMPOWER

Leaving a positive footprint wherever you go is about setting standards for others to follow. Ask yourself how you make people feel after they've been in your company or spoken with you. Not all conversations are positive, but you can influence how people feel afterward. Take pride in empowering others to be their best and inspiring them to feel energized after being with you. This is a trait of those who truly demonstrate excellence.

CHALLENGE:

Reflect on a recent interaction you had with someone. Consider how you made that person feel during and after the conversation. Think about ways you can leave a more positive footprint in future interactions. Make a conscious effort to empower and inspire those you meet, ensuring they feel valued and energized by your presence.

CONTENTMENT VS. COMPLACENCY: UNDERSTAND THE DIFFERENCE

Understanding the balance between contentment and complacency is crucial. Contentment means being satisfied and at peace with what you have. Complacency, on the other hand, means feeling no need to improve or strive for more. Often, we mistake complacency for contentment, believing we are content when we are merely complacent. Recognizing the difference is essential because complacency is the greatest enemy of success, while contentment is the art of appreciating and enjoying what's truly best.

CHALLENGE:

Examine an area of your life where you might be feeling complacent. Ask yourself if you are truly content or if you are avoiding challenges. Identify one action you can take to move beyond complacency while still appreciating the simplicity and joy of contentment. See how finding this balance helps you grow and achieve success without losing your sense of happiness.

MAKE CHOICES: DECIDE WITH PURPOSE

Every decision we make, big or small, shapes our path and determines our outcomes. The power to choose our attitude, actions, and responses to life's challenges empowers us to take control of our own destiny. It's not about the circumstances we face, but how we choose to respond to them that matters. When we make decisions that align with our goals, values, and dreams, we navigate our lives in the direction we desire.

CHALLENGE:

Identify one upcoming decision and take the time to consider its potential impact. Be clear on your choice, evaluate the potential outcomes, and commit fully to your decision. Confident and committed decision-making will always move you forward in a positive direction.

THE WEIGHT OF W.O.P.T.O.M: FREE YOURSELF

W.O.P.T.O.M – What Other People Think Of Me. No matter how confident or successful you are, at some point you will find yourself directing your energy towards W.O.P.T.O.M.

It's one of life's greatest energy vampires, fueling doubt and concern based on little fact or evidence. W.O.P.T.O.M is a self-made perception that misdirects your energy and justifies your thoughts, feelings, and actions.

People will always have opinions. It's important not to try to read minds because you're probably wrong.

CHALLENGE:

Identify a recent situation where you were concerned about what others thought. Reflect on whether your concern was based on fact or assumption. Focus on your values and actions instead of others' opinions. Notice how freeing yourself from W.O.P.T.O.M redirects your energy towards positive actions.

PURSUE EXCELLENCE: STRIVE FOR THE BEST

Excellence is about striving to be the best version of yourself. It means putting in the effort, going the extra mile, and constantly looking for ways to improve. Daily excellence is a personal responsibility; it requires commitment, the right attitude, respect for the process, and understanding that excellence is a full-time position, not a part-time role. Remember to C.A.R.E: Commitment > Attitude > Respect > Excellence.

CHALLENGE:

Reflect on the concept of C.A.R.E... Identify one action you can take today to demonstrate commitment, a positive attitude, respect for the process, or excellence in what you do. Implement this action and see how it influences your day and interactions with others. Anything worth achieving isn't easy, but it's worth the effort. Embracing excellence in small, everyday actions contributes to your overall growth and success.

STORIES THAT LEAVE A FOOTPRINT

STORY 4: PURSUING EXCELLENCE

Severiano Ballesteros, one of golf's greatest and most influential figures of his time, was not only my childhood hero but also became a great friend and mentor who significantly influenced my coaching career. Seve often shared valuable insights and stories that have stayed with me throughout my career.

I was lucky to share and exchange many stories with Seve, and one particular story stands out. It was the 1984 British Open, where Seve's infamous fist pump after holing his putt on the 18th still raises the hairs on the back of my neck to this day. Seve emphasized that sheer will and determination surpass skill. His intense desire to succeed in that moment turned a challenging putt into a winning shot. Despite the immense pressure, his unwavering focus and willpower carried him through.

This story teaches us that excellence is driven by an inner resolve to succeed, beyond mere talent. Seve's journey and wisdom have profoundly shaped my approach to coaching, reminding me and my athletes that true success comes from within.

Lesson: True excellence is achieved through an unwavering will and determination, driving you to overcome obstacles and succeed.

Footprint: "You Are Where Your Feet Are" - by being fully present and committed in the moment, your current resolve and focus are what push you toward excellence.

"*EXCELLENCE IS NOT A SKILL, IT'S AN ATTITUDE.*".

———

RALPH MARSTON

NOTES & REFLECTIONS

What new things have you discovered about yourself?

How have these challenges developed the way you think and act?

What new things have you discovered about yourself?

How have these challenges developed the way you think and act?

What new things have you discovered about yourself?

How have these challenges developed the way you think and act?

What new things have you discovered about yourself?

How have these challenges developed the way you think and act?

What new things have you discovered about yourself?

How have these challenges developed the way you think and act?

REFERENCE GUIDE: "YOU ARE WHERE YOUR FEET ARE"

This reference guide is designed to help you revisit and reflect on the challenges and lessons you've encountered in "You Are Where Your Feet Are." Use this guide to reinforce your growth and keep track of the valuable insights you've gained.

1. Navigate Uncertainty: Find Your Path

Challenge: Identify an area of uncertainty in your life, list possible paths forward, and choose one step to clarify your direction.

2. Embrace Change: Adapt and Grow

Challenge: Reflect on a recent change, identify a positive aspect, and write down how you adapted and what you learned.

3. Discover Purpose: Find Meaning

Challenge: Write down what brings you happiness and satisfaction, reflect on moments of engagement, and align your actions with your core values.

4. Practice Patience: Take It Step by Step

Challenge: Break a goal into smaller tasks, focus on completing one task daily, and reflect on how this routine helps you stay on track.

5. Show Gratitude: Appreciate Each Step

Challenge: Share three things you're grateful for each day and reflect on how this practice influences your perspective.

6. Build Relationships: Connect with Others

Challenge: Reconnect with someone you haven't spoken to in a while and reflect on the mutual benefits of this renewed connection.

7. Manage Stress: Lighten Your Load

Challenge: Identify a source of stress, develop a strategy to reduce its impact, and implement changes to improve your well-being.

8. Be Open-Minded: Embrace Diversity

Challenge: Engage in conversations with people from different backgrounds and reflect on how these interactions broaden your perspective.

9. Take Initiative: Take Action

Challenge: Identify an area where you've been waiting for things to happen, take the first step towards progress, and reflect on how this helps you gain control.

10. Develop Resilience: Bounce Back Stronger

Challenge: Reflect on a recent challenge, identify a valuable lesson, and apply it to handle future challenges more effectively.

11. Seek Balance: Find Harmony

Challenge: Assess your schedule, identify an imbalanced area, and make a specific adjustment to create more balance.

12. Creativity: Explore Ideas

Challenge: Dedicate time to a creative hobby or project and reflect on how this enhances your curiosity and personal growth.

13. Communication: Understand and Be Understood

Challenge: Practice active listening in a crucial relationship and reflect on how this improves your interactions.

14. Integrity: Be Honest and True

Challenge: Reflect on your core values, demonstrate integrity in your actions, and notice how this enhances your relationships and self-respect.

15. Inspire Others: Motivate and Encourage

Challenge: Reach out to someone who needs support, offer words of encouragement, and reflect on the impact of your efforts.

16. Celebrate Success: Acknowledge Achievements

Challenge: Reflect on a recent accomplishment, reward yourself, and notice how this celebration boosts your morale.

17. Learn from Failure: Grow from Mistakes

Challenge: Think of a recent failure, identify a key lesson, and apply this knowledge to improve future actions.

18. Nurture Compassion: Be Kind to Yourself

Challenge: Replace self-critical thoughts with words of self-compassion and dedicate time to self-care activities.

19. Challenge Assumptions: Question What You Know

Challenge: Identify a belief, seek different perspectives, and reflect on how this changes or confirms your view.

20. Choose Courage: Be Brave

Challenge: Confront a fear or concern, take a small step towards overcoming it, and reflect on the impact on your confidence.

21. Reflect Regularly: Pause and Contemplate

Challenge: Schedule regular reflection time, write down your thoughts, and use these insights to guide your actions and decisions.

22. Take Control: Move Your Feet to Where They Need to Be

Challenge: Identify an area where you feel stuck, write down three small steps to move forward, and take the first step today.

23. Prepare for Success: Plan Ahead

Challenge: Identify a goal, write down your intention, steps, and emotional management plan, and set simple milestones.

24. Trust the Process: Believe in the Journey

Challenge: Break down a task into small, manageable chunks and focus on completing one step at a time.

25. Invest in Yourself: Personal Growth

Challenge: Identify an area for self-investment, dedicate time and resources, and notice the positive impact on your wellbeing.

26. Leave a Positive Footprint: Inspire and Empower

Challenge: Reflect on a recent interaction, consider how you made the person feel, and make an effort to empower and inspire others.

27. Contentment vs. Complacency: Know the Difference

Challenge: Identify an area where you might be complacent, push yourself out of complacency, and appreciate contentment.

28. Make Choices: Decide with Purpose

Challenge: Identify an upcoming decision, consider its impact, and commit fully to your choice.

29. The Weight of W.O.P.T.O.M: Free Yourself

Challenge: Reflect on a situation where you were concerned about others' opinions, focus on your values, and free yourself from W.O.P.T.O.M.

30. Pursue Excellence: Strive for the Best

Challenge: Reflect on C.A.R.E (Commitment, Attitude, Respect, Excellence), identify an action to demonstrate these qualities, and implement it.

IS THIS BOOK FOR YOU?

"You Are Where Your Feet Are" is for anyone who wants to maximize their present moment and strive for personal excellence. This fun, fast, and easy read provides practical tools and insights to help you change behavior and develop habits of excellence.

Whether you're navigating career challenges, leading teams, inspiring others, managing responsibilities, or simply seeking daily improvement, this book offers the guidance you need.

Embrace your current situation, make the most of every moment, and cultivate habits that lead to lasting success. "You Are Where Your Feet Are" will empower you to live purposefully and effectively, no matter where you are on your journey.